Welcome to the wonderful world of music making. Your teacher has shown you how to hold your instrument and make a sound on the mouthpiece. Let's begin learning some song

You can find play-a-long mp3s for the first part of this book at **www.m**

1. Our First Note

2. Our Second Note

3. Three's a Crowd

4. Four In a Row

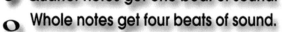

Quarter notes get one beat of sound.
Whole notes get four beats of sound.

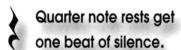

Quarter note rests get one beat of silence.

5. A Funny Pair

6. Skate Board Sam

7. Catch That Note

8. Keep On Blowin'

9. Our Third Note   NEW NOTE "F"

10. Couch Potato

11. Puppy Dogs

12. Our Fourth Note   NEW NOTE   "C"

13. Apple for the Teacher

14. Our Fifth Note   NEW NOTE   "Bb"

15. Bumper Cars

4

 **Half Note**

Two Beats of Sound

16. Half Notes Happen

17. Hot Cross Buns

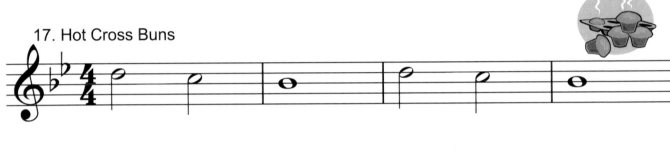

Notes are written on lines and spaces called the "staff".

How many lines can you find?
How many spaces can you find?

18. High Dive

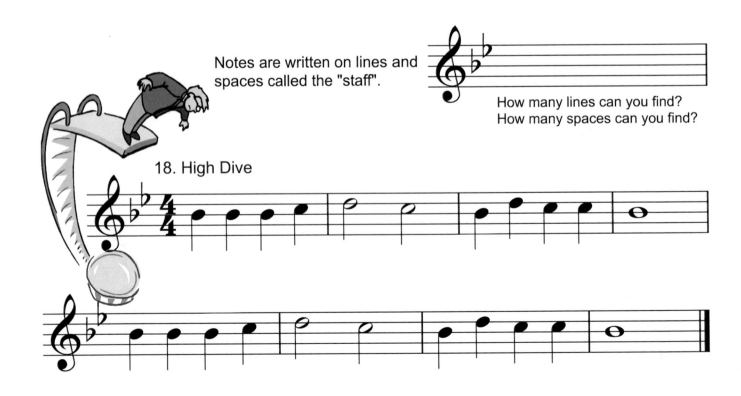

6

22. Notes I Love

NEW NOTE "A"

23. Shoo Fly, Don't Bother Me!

24. Crazy Tonguing

Rhythm Fun

Eighth Notes

One eighth note gets 1/2 count.
Two eighth notes get ONE count.

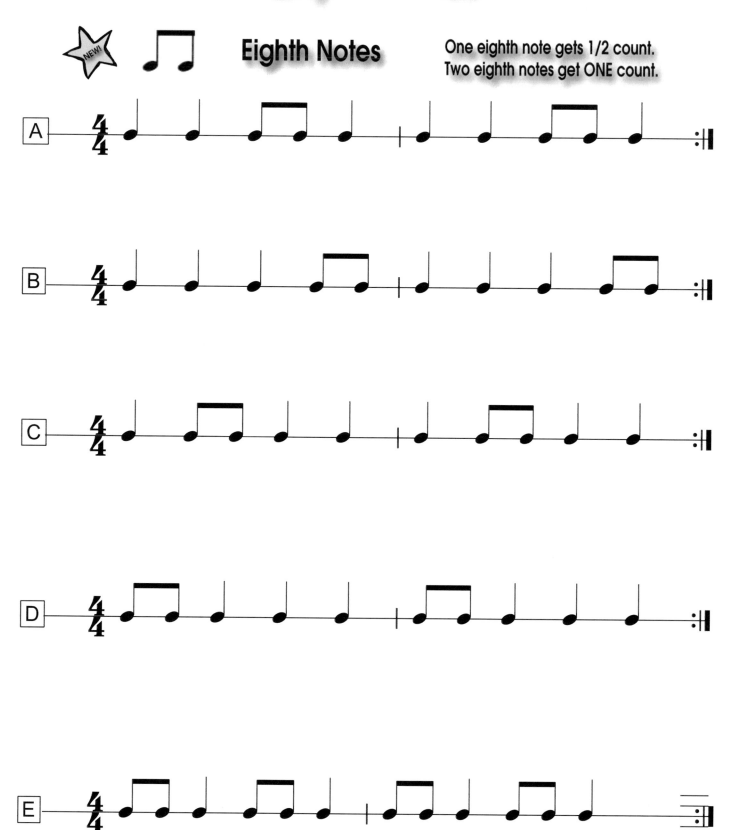

25. Yankee Doodle Cha Cha

26. Caribbean Cruise

27. Country Hoe Down

28. Eighth Note Slide

Repeat Sign

NEW!

A double bar with TWO DOTS at the end of the measure tell you to REPEAT the music.

29. The Cabbage Song

NEW! NEW NOTE "G"

30. Old MacDonald Had a Farm

Half note rests get
two beats of silence.

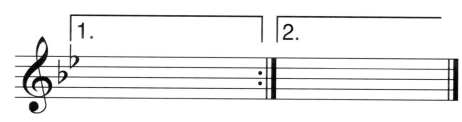

First and Second Endings

When you reach the repeat sign under the first ending, stop and go back to the beginning. When you get to the first ending again, skip it and go to the second ending.

31. Stodola Pumpa

32. London Bridge

 **Slur**

A "slur" is a curved line that connects two or more notes of different pitches. Tongue the first note and move to the next notes without tonguing. Don't stop blowing.

 Tie

A "tie" is a curved line that connects two or more notes of the same pitch. Hold the note for the combined value of the notes.

 Dotted Half Note

A dotted half note gets three beats of sound.

33. Southern Roses

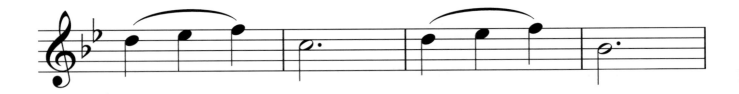

Pick-Up Notes

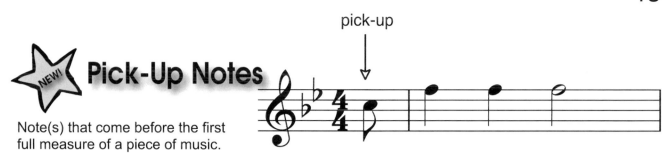

Note(s) that come before the first full measure of a piece of music.

Fermata (Hold)

Hold (keep blowing) the note until your director tells you to stop,

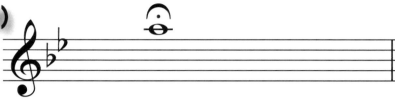

34. Snake Charmer

35. Aura Lee

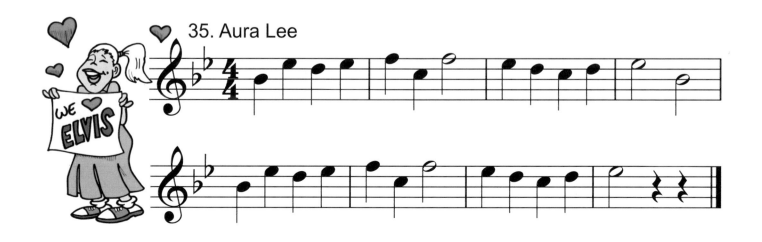

14

36. Jingle Bells

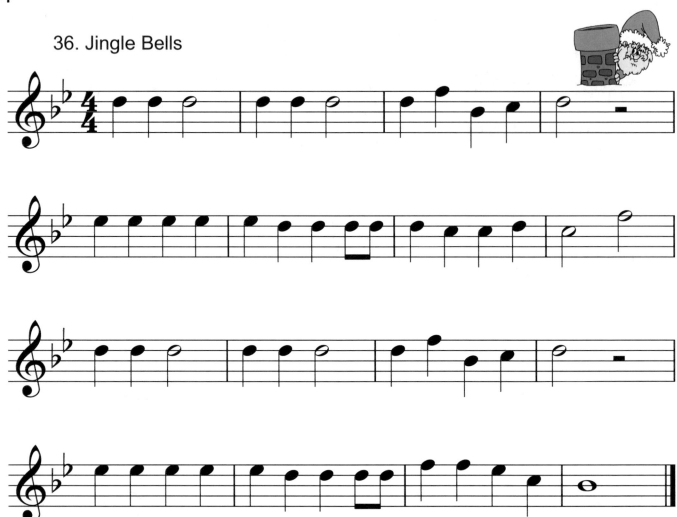

D.C. al Fine

Go back to the beginning and play until "Fine".

37. Twinkle, Twinkle, Little Star

D.S. al Fine

Go back to the sign and play until "Fine".

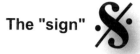

The "sign"

38. Ode to Joy

Fine

D.S. al Fine

Flat Sign

♭

NEW NOTE **"Ab"**

A "flat" lowers the note one half step. It stays in effect for the entire measure.

39. Yankee Doodle

Time Signature

A "time signature" tells you how many beats there are in each measure of music.

40. Little Cabin in the Wood

Key Signature

A "key signature" changes certain notes throughout a piece of music.

When you see this key signature, play all the B's, E's and A's as FLATS.

41. It's a Ringer!

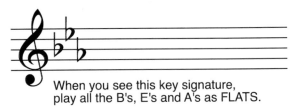

42. Polly Wolly Doodle

Natural Sign

A "natural" cancels a sharp or flat. It remains in effect for the entire measure.

NEW NOTE

"E Natural"

43. Mary's Other Lamb

44. O Come Little Children (Melody)

45. O Come Little Children (Harmony)

18

Dynamics

p Piano
Play with a soft volume.

f Forte
Play with a full volume.

50. Minka, Minka

51. Rollin' Back and Forth

Your left hand remains the same.
Your right hand does all the work.

Dotted Quarter Note

A dotted quarter note gets one and one half counts.

52. America

53. Technical Foul

Rhythm Fun

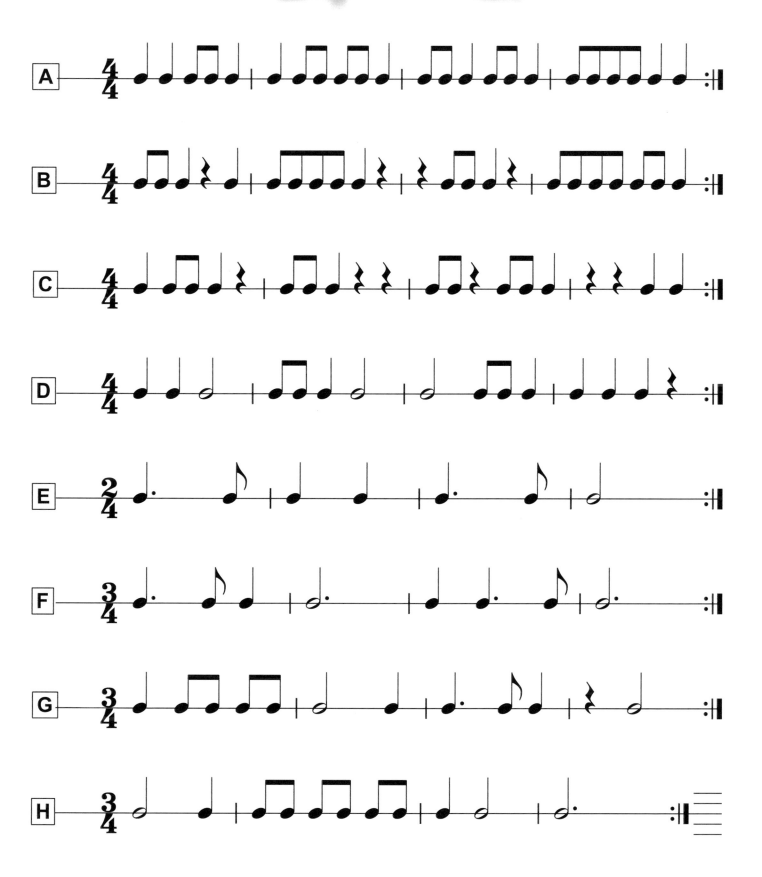

22

54. Rhythm Wreck

NEW NOTE Low "A" flat is fingered the same as your other "A" flat. Blow easy.

"Low Ab"

55. More Hot Cross Buns

NEW! **Natural Sign** A natural sign cancels a flat or a sharp. It remains in effect for the entire measure.

56. It Just Comes Naturally

57. Don't Be Fooled

Accent Sign

> An accent sign tells you to play the note with more emphasis.

 Eighth Rest

An eighth rest gets one half beat of silence.

58. Go, Fight, Win

59. Bach Minuet

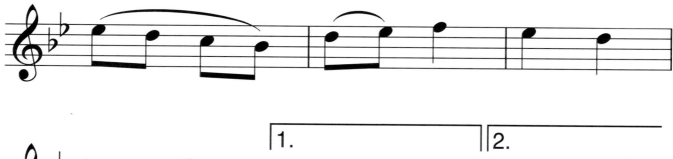

24

60. Rueben and Rachel

61. When Love is Kind

Dynamics

mp Mezzo Piano
Play with a medium soft volume.

mf Mezzo Forte
Play with a medium loud volume.

62. Mexican Hat Dance

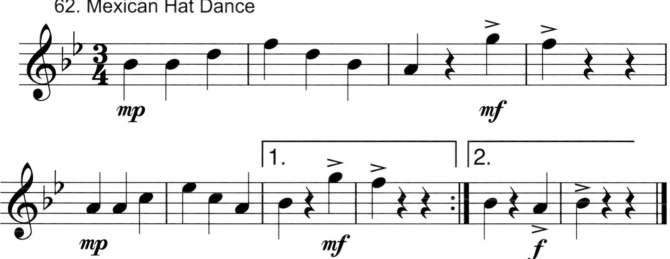

63. Blues Dues

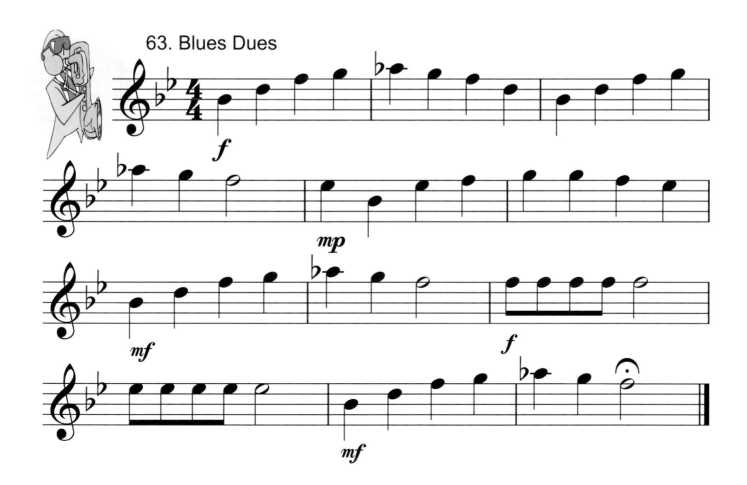

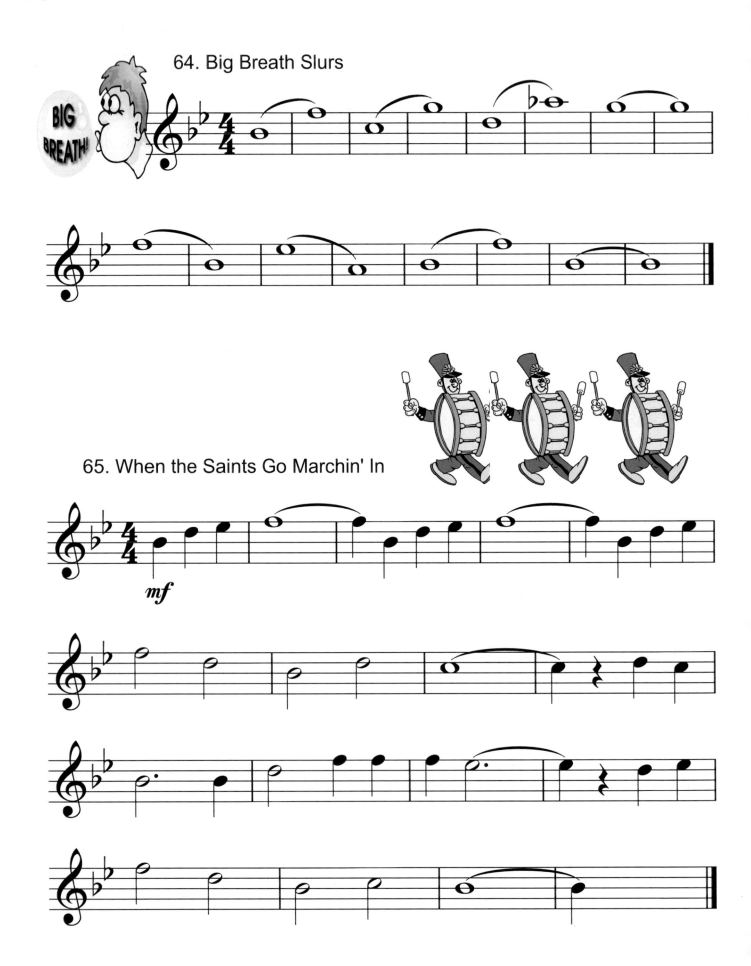

64. Big Breath Slurs

65. When the Saints Go Marchin' In

mf

28

69. Danger! Tricky Rhythms

70. Bye, Baby Bunting

Decrescendo — Get softer

Crescendo Get louder

71. Monster Melodies

Sharp Sign
♯

A "SHARP" raises a note one half step.
It remains in effect for the entire measure.

NEW NOTE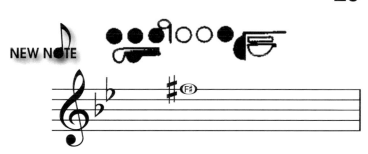

72. Barcarolle

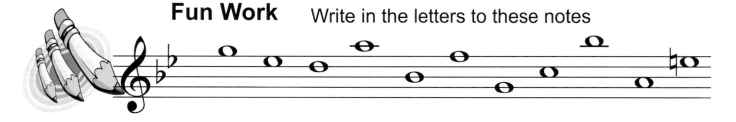

Fun Work   Write in the letters to these notes

Special Page for Flutes

The Alternate "B flat" Fingering

Use the second fingering indicated for the
alternate way to play the "B flat".

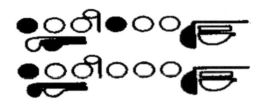 

Use the alternate thumb lever throughout.

Octave Workout

High C

High D

Moving Higher

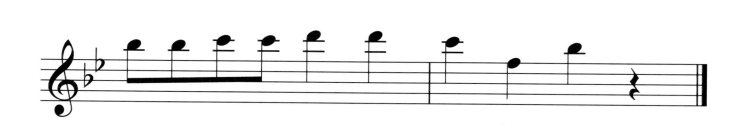

More Octave Workouts

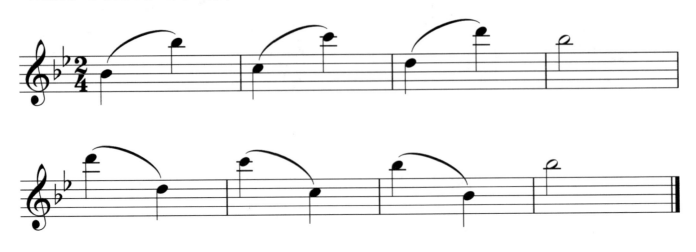

Long Tones

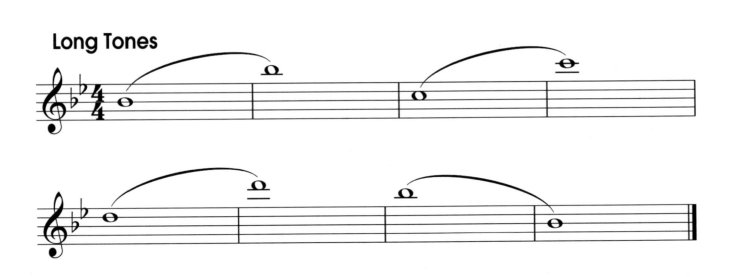

73. Can Can

74. La Bamba

34

75. Simple Gifts

76. Amazing Grace

Complete the Story Game

_____ (1) and her mom and _____ (2) were moving into a new home at the

_____ (3) of town. It was there last night in the old house. Everything was moved out

except for a few boxes, a _____ (4), some _____ (5) and a sleeping _____ (6).

_____ (7) said, "It sure is _____ (8) around here." She _____ (9) to have a party

that last night, but _____ (10) said it was a _____ (11) time to have friends over, and, also

it was late. Mom _____ (12) that there was no way she could _____ (13) anyone, so

a party was out.

Just then the door flew open. There were Ruthie, _____ (14) and _____ (15) standing in

the doorway, yelling "Surprise!" Each carried a _____ (16) filled with goodies. They also

brought paper plates and cups. There was even a jug of lemon _____ (17). What started

out as a dull evening turned out to be a fun time for all.

Name Your Friends

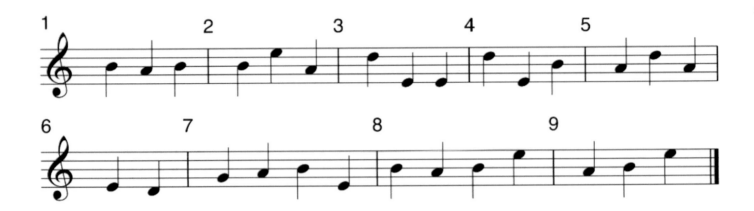

The measures above spell names. Find all the names and then pretend that the kids below are your music friends. Give each person a name.

Congratutions on completing the first half of this book.

The remainder of the book will focus on more intermediate level material that will take you to the next level of music performance with additional scales, technical exercises and new songs. Keep up the great work!

Bb Major Scale Review (Bb Concert)

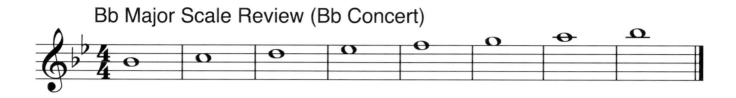

Eb Major Scale Review (Eb Concert)

Southern Roses

Ode to Joy

38

Bb Major Scale

Bb Major Scale Study

Bb Major Arpeggio

Haydn's Theme from the London Symphony

Barcarolle

Offenbach

41

42

Slurring Up and Down

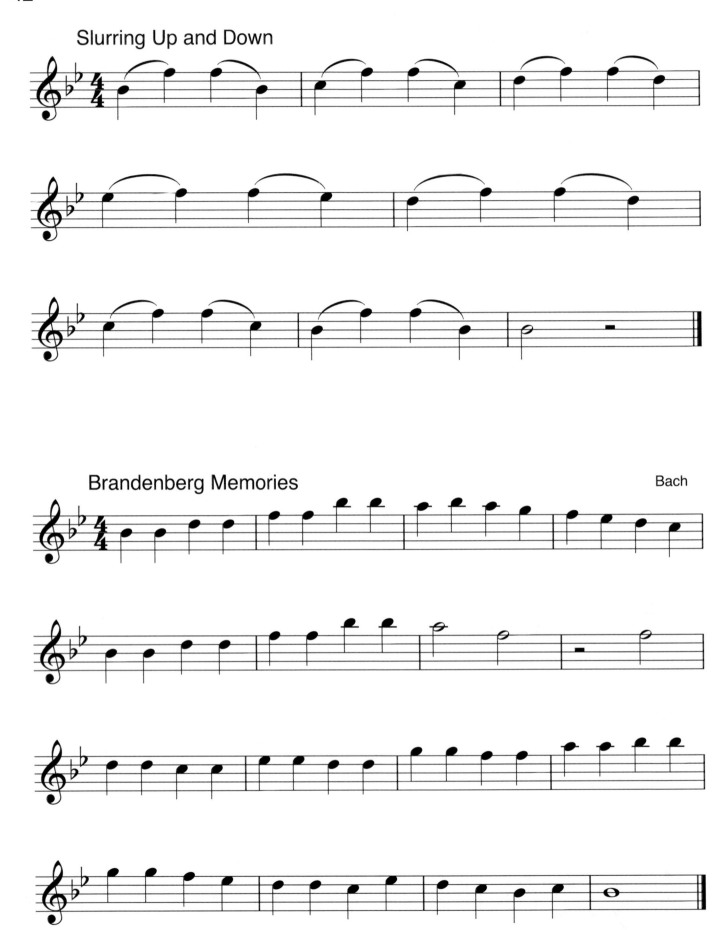

Brandenberg Memories

Bach

Eb Major Scale

Eb Major Review

Eb Major Etude

Eb Major Upper Octave

Eb Major Arpeggio

Russian Folk Song

Beethoven

Eb Major Scale Etude

Blues Dues

Eb Major Arpeggio Etude

Ab Major Scale Study

Ab Major Scale

Buffalo Gals

John Hodges

mf

Ab Major Scale Etude

Ab Major Jumping Jacks

Arpeggios in Ab Major

48

Hatikvah

mf

Pattern Changes

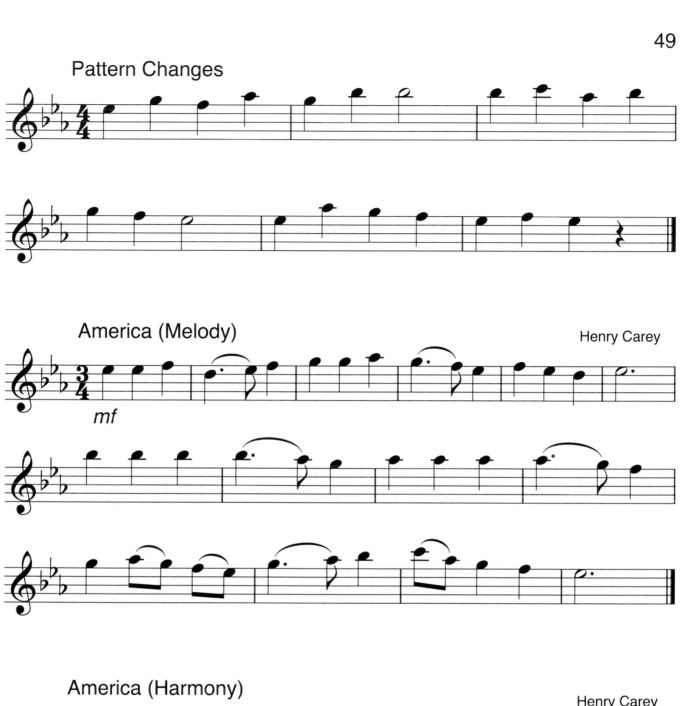

America (Melody)

Henry Carey

America (Harmony)

Henry Carey

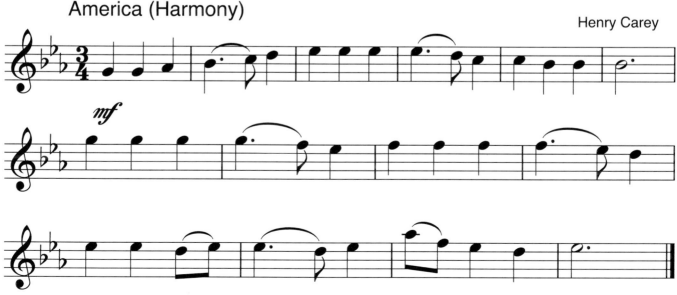

Surprise Symphony

Haydn

When Love Is Kind

Irish Folk Song

Eb Major Jumping Jacks

Carnival Ride

Movin' Upwards

Sakura

Japanese Folk Song

The Road Up the Hill

F Major Scale Study

F Major Arpeggio Study

Don't Mess with the Man

Dotted Quarter Rhythms

Dotted Quarter Slurs

Arirang

Korean Folk Song

54

Little Waltz

Mozart

All Through the Night

Welsh Folk Song

The Sandman

German Folk Song

Get Set to Accent

Accent City

Sitka City

Russian Folk Song

Mexican Hat Dance

Traditional

Frolic

Anonymous

C Major Scale

Jubilate

Mozart

mf

Happy Little Donkey

Round

Slovakian Folk Song

58

D Major Scale

The Chase

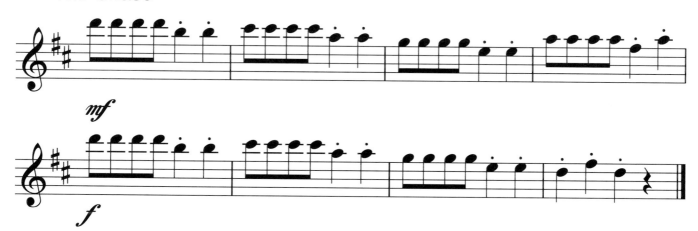

Rakes of Mallow (Version One)

Irish Folk Song

Rakes of Mallow (Version Two)

Irish Folk Song

60

Bb Minor Scale (Harmonic)

Bb Minor Scale (Melodic)

Bb Minor Arpeggio

Bb Minor Waltz

Shalom Chaverim

Hebrew Folk Song

Sixteenth Note Dance

Sixteenth Note Run

Movin' Fast

Dinah, Won't You Blow Your Horn

Runnin' Round Town

Tirra Lirra Loo

Canadian Folk Song

American Patrol

Meacham

Oats and Beans

Skip to My Lou

American Folk Song

Theme from "Concerto in A Minor" (First Movement)

Vivaldi

Movin' Fast

Syncopation Song

Syncopation Scale

Syncopation March

Who Built the Ark?

Bahamamian Folk Song

Syncopation Hook

6/8 Time March

6/8 Scale

Row, Row, Row Your Boat

Round

mf   cresc.

f   decresc.   *mf*

Follow the Old Brick Road

For He's a Jolly Good Fellow

mf

Eb Minor Scale (Low)

Eb Minor Scale (High)

Eb Minor Melodic Minor Study

Russian Sailor's Dance

Gilere

Gypsy Dance

Russian Folk Song

68

The Chromatic Scale

Habañera

Bizet

Low or High?

Chromatic Waltz

Follow the Old Brick Road

Left and Right

6/8 Time Scale

I Saw Three Ships

English Carol

70

Joshua Fought the Battle of Jericho

African-American Spiritual

Unfinished Symphony

Schubert

Turkish March

Beethoven

Anchor's Aweigh

Capt. A.H. Miles & C.A. Zimmerman

March from the Nutcracker

Tchaikovsky

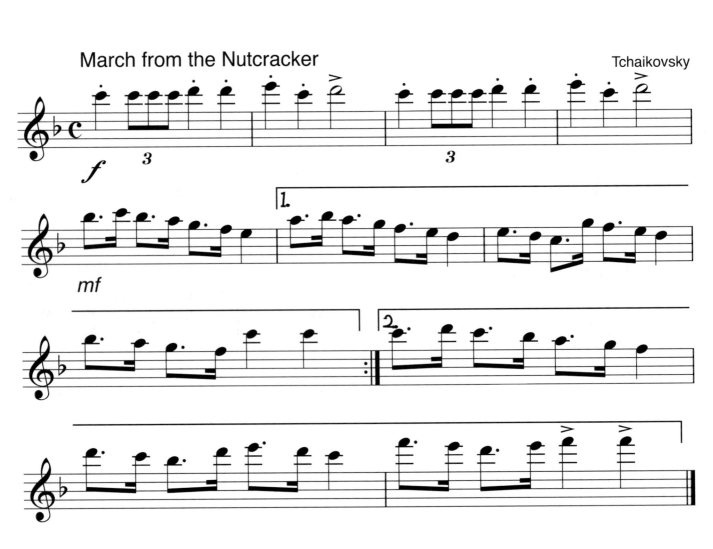

The Star-Spangled Banner

U.S. National Anthem

O Canada

Canadian National Anthem

DUET SECTION

Aura Lee

Camptown Races

Camptown Races

Mozart Processional

Mozart Processional

Amazing Grace

Amazing Grace

Angels We Have Heard on High

Angels We Have Heard on High

Chanukah Medley

Chanukah Medley

Harmony

Brahm's Lullaby

Melody

Brahm's Lullaby

Harmony

Turkey in the Straw
American Folk Song

Old MacDonald

Old MacDonald

Pomp and Circumstance

Elgar

Pomp and Circumstance

Elgar

Holiday Medley (*melody*)

Holiday Medley (*harmony*)

Hunter's Chorus (*melody*)

von Weber

Hunter's Chorus (*harmony*)

von Weber

TRIO SECTION
Cassion Song

The Bridge at Avignon

Pop Goes the Weasel

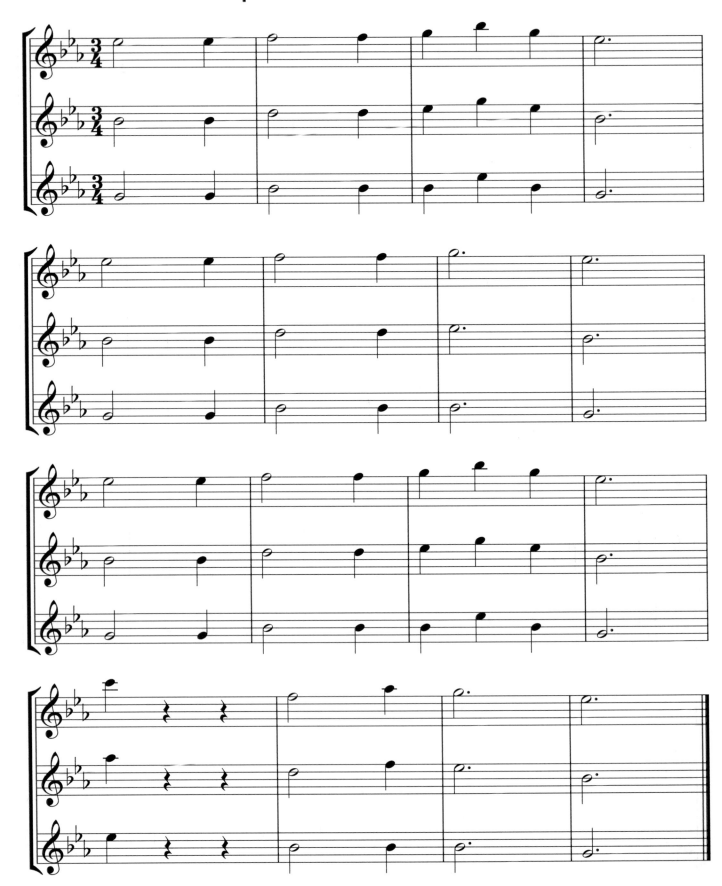

Jingle Bells

This Little Light of Mine

Up on the House Top

Spring Theme from the Four Seasons

Kum Ba Yah

Ode to Joy

Oh, Susana

Shepherd's Hey

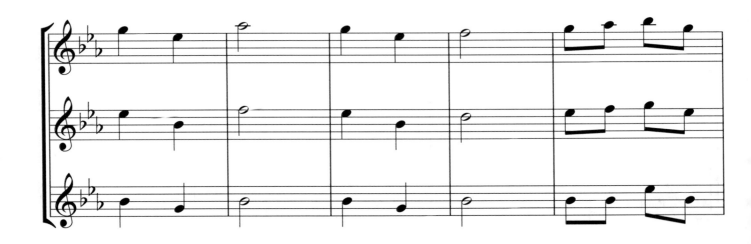

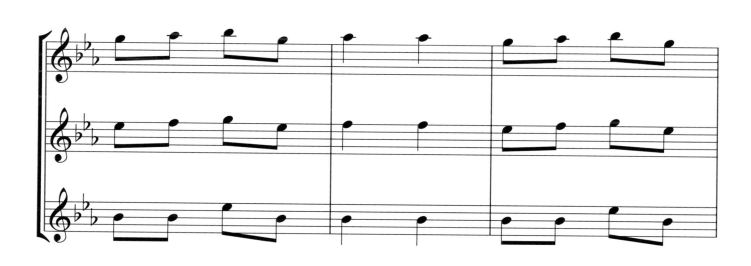

Flute Fingering Chart